Mastering Prompt Engineering: Unlocking the Power of Language Models

Table of Contents

Designing Effective Prompts

1. Components of a Prompt

2. Crafting Clear and Concise Prompts

3. Context and Relevance in Prompt Design

4. Techniques for Prompt Refinement

5. Examples of Good and Bad Prompts

Advanced Prompt Engineering Techniques

1. Dynamic Prompt Generation

2. Conditional and Contextual Prompts

3. Using Prompts for Zero-Shot and Few-Shot

   Learning

4. Prompt Optimization Strategies

2. Using OpenAI's API for Prompt Design

3. Utilizing Hugging Face Transformers

4. Custom Tools and Scripts for Prompt

   Management

Testing and Evaluating Prompts

1. Metrics for Prompt Evaluation

2. A/B Testing for Prompt Performance

3. User Feedback and Prompt Iteration

4. Case Studies of Prompt Testing and

   Improvement

Challenges and Best Practices

1. Common Issues in Prompt Engineering

Introduction to Prompt Engineering

What is Prompt Engineering?

Prompt engineering is the practice of designing and refining input prompts to maximize the performance and utility of language models (LLMs) like GPT-4, BERT, and T5. This involves crafting precise and effective instructions that guide the model to generate the desired output.

Importance of Prompts in LLMs

Prompts are crucial in LLMs as they directly influence the quality, relevance, and accuracy of the model's output. Well-engineered prompts can improve model performance, ensuring that

responses are useful and aligned with user

expectations.

Applications of Prompt Engineering

Prompt engineering is applied in various domains:

- **Chatbots and Conversational Agents:** Enhancing user interaction with intelligent responses.

- **Content Generation:** Creating articles, summaries, and other textual content.

- **Sentiment Analysis:** Extracting opinions and sentiments from text data.

- **Question Answering:** Providing accurate and relevant answers to user queries.

- **Code Generation:** Assisting in programming and code completion tasks.

- **Personalized Recommendations:** Tailoring responses and recommendations to individual users.

Overview of Popular LLMs

- **GPT (Generative Pre-trained Transformer):** Known for its conversational abilities and text generation.

- **BERT (Bidirectional Encoder Representations from Transformers):** Excels in understanding the context of words in sentences for tasks like Q&A.

- **T5 (Text-To-Text Transfer Transformer):** Converts various NLP tasks into a text-to-text format, enhancing flexibility.

Fundamentals of Prompt Engineering

Understanding LLMs and Their Capabilities

LLMs are pre-trained on vast amounts of text data and can perform a wide range of language-related tasks. They generate outputs based on the input prompts, leveraging their training to understand and respond appropriately.

Key Concepts and Terminology

- **Prompt:** The input text given to an LLM to generate a response.

- **Zero-Shot Learning:** The model performs a task without explicit task-specific examples.

- **Few-Shot Learning:** The model is given a few examples to understand the task.

- **Context:** Additional information provided to help the model generate relevant outputs.

Basic Principles of Effective Prompts

- **Clarity:** Use clear and straightforward language.

- **Specificity:** Provide specific instructions to avoid ambiguity.

- **Relevance:** Ensure the prompt is relevant to the desired output.

Differences in Prompt Design for GPT, BERT, T5, and Others

- **GPT:** Focus on natural, conversational prompts.

- **BERT:** Utilize prompts that require understanding context and relationships.

- **T5:** Frame tasks as text transformations, using a uniform input-output format.

Designing Effective Prompts

Components of a Prompt

- **Instruction:** Clear guidelines on what is expected.

- **Context:** Background information to guide the response.

- **Examples:** Illustrative instances to clarify expectations.

Crafting Clear and Concise Prompts

Clear prompts lead to better responses. For instance:

- **Bad Prompt:** "Write about dogs."

- **Good Prompt:** "Write a 200-word article about the benefits of owning a dog."

Context and Relevance in Prompt Design

Providing context helps models understand and generate relevant responses. For example:

- **With Context:** "In a conversation about pet care, explain the benefits of owning a dog."

Techniques for Prompt Refinement

- **Iteration:** Continuously refine prompts based on model performance.

- **Feedback:** Incorporate user feedback to improve prompt quality.

- **Testing:** Experiment with different prompt variations.

Examples of Good and Bad Prompts

- **Bad Prompt:** "Tell me a story."

- **Good Prompt:** "Tell me a short story about a brave knight who saves a village from a dragon."

Advanced Prompt Engineering Techniques

Dynamic Prompt Generation

Creating prompts that adapt based on user input or contextual changes can enhance interactions.

Conditional and Contextual Prompts

Designing prompts that change based on specific conditions or contexts to provide more relevant responses.

Using Prompts for Zero-Shot and Few-Shot Learning

- **Zero-Shot Example:** "Translate the following English text to French: 'Hello, how are you?'"

- **Few-Shot Example:** Providing a couple of translation examples before asking for a new translation.

Prompt Optimization Strategies

- **Hyperparameter Tuning:** Adjust parameters influencing model behavior.

- **Prompt Templates:** Develop reusable templates for consistent results.

Incorporating Feedback and Iteration

Regularly gather and apply feedback to refine and improve prompts.

Prompt Engineering for Specific Use Cases

Chatbots and Conversational Agents

Crafting prompts that ensure engaging and contextually appropriate conversations.

Example

- **Prompt:** "As a friendly chatbot, introduce yourself to a new user and ask how you can assist them today."

Content Generation and Summarization

Generating informative and concise content based on input data.

Example

- **Prompt:** "Summarize the key points of the following article in 100 words."

Sentiment Analysis and Opinion Mining

Extracting sentiments and opinions from text data.

Example

- **Prompt:** "Analyze the sentiment of the following review and categorize it as positive, negative, or neutral."

Question Answering and Information Retrieval

Providing accurate answers to specific questions based on context.

Example

- **Prompt:** "Based on the provided text, answer the question: 'What are the main benefits of renewable energy?'"

Code Generation and Programming Assistance

Assisting in writing and debugging code.

Example

- **Prompt:** "Generate a Python function to sort a list of integers in ascending order."

Personalized Recommendations and User Interaction

Tailoring responses to individual preferences and needs.

Example

- **Prompt:** "Based on the user's reading history, suggest three books they might enjoy."

Tools and Frameworks for Prompt Engineering

Overview of Prompt Engineering Tools

- **OpenAI's API:** Provides access to models like GPT-4 for prompt-based tasks.

- **Hugging Face Transformers:** Offers a range of pre-trained models and tools for NLP tasks.

Using OpenAI's API for Prompt Design

Example Code

python

Copy code

```
import openai

openai.api_key = 'your-api-key'
```

```python
response = openai.Completion.create(
    model="text-davinci-003",
    prompt="Write a poem about the sea.",
    max_tokens=50
)

print(response.choices[0].text.strip())
```

Utilizing Hugging Face Transformers

Example Code

python

Copy code

```python
from transformers import pipeline
```

```python
generator = pipeline('text-generation',

model='gpt-2')

response = generator("Once upon a time",

max_length=50)


print(response[0]['generated_text'])
```

Custom Tools and Scripts for Prompt Management

Developing scripts to automate prompt testing and optimization.

Testing and Evaluating Prompts

Metrics for Prompt Evaluation

- **Accuracy:** Correctness of the response.

- **Relevance:** Appropriateness of the response to the prompt.

- **Fluency:** Naturalness and readability of the response.

A/B Testing for Prompt Performance

Comparing different prompts to identify which performs better.

User Feedback and Prompt Iteration

Collecting and analyzing user feedback to improve

prompts iteratively.

Challenges and Best Practices

Common Issues in Prompt Engineering

- **Ambiguity:** Vague prompts leading to unclear responses.

- **Bias:** Unintended bias in prompts affecting responses.

- **Overfitting:** Prompts too narrowly tailored, limiting flexibility.

Ethical Considerations and Bias in Prompts

Ensuring prompts do not reinforce stereotypes or discriminatory behavior.

Ensuring Robustness and Scalability

Designing prompts that maintain performance across different contexts and scales.

Best Practices for Continuous Improvement

- **Regular Review:** Continuously evaluate prompt effectiveness.

- **User Involvement:** Incorporate user insights in prompt refinement.

Future Trends in Prompt Engineering

Emerging Technologies and Techniques

- **Adaptive Prompts:** Utilizing real-time data to adjust prompts dynamically.

- **Multimodal Prompts:** Combining text with other data types (e.g., images, audio).

The Future of Interactive AI

Enhanced interaction capabilities through improved prompt engineering.

Research Directions and Innovations

Exploring new methodologies to further advance prompt effectiveness.

Preparing for Future Developments

Staying informed about the latest trends and tools in prompt engineering.

Conclusion

Recap of Key Learnings

Prompt engineering is essential for maximizing the utility of LLMs, involving careful design, testing, and refinement of prompts to achieve desired outcomes.

Final Thoughts on Prompt Engineering

Effective prompt engineering requires continuous learning, adaptation, and ethical considerations to harness the full potential of language models